Occupational Safety and Health Act of 1970
"To assure safe and healthful working conditions for
working men and women; by authorizing enforcement
of the standards developed under the Act; by assisting
and encouraging the States in their efforts to assure
safe and healthful working conditions; by providing for
research, information, education, and training in the field
of occupational safety and health..."

This publication provides a general overview of worker rights
under the *Occupational Safety and Health Act* (OSH Act).
This publication does not alter or determine compliance
responsibilities which are set forth in OSHA standards and the
OSH Act. Moreover, because interpretations and enforcement
policy may change over time, for additional guidance on OSHA
compliance requirements the reader should consult current
administrative interpretations and decisions by the Occupational
Safety and Health Review Commission and the courts.

This information will be made available to sensory-impaired
individuals upon request. Voice phone: (202) 693-1999;
teletypewriter (TTY) number: 1-877-889-5627.

Guidelines for Preventing Workplace Violence for Healthcare and Social Service Workers

U.S. Department of Labor
Occupational Safety and Health Administration

OSHA 3148-04R 2015

U.S. Department of Labor

Table of Contents

Overview of the Guidelines

Healthcare and social service workers face significant risks of job-related violence and it is OSHA's mission to help employers address these serious hazards. This publication updates OSHA's 1996 and 2004 voluntary guidelines for preventing workplace violence for healthcare and social service workers. OSHA's violence prevention guidelines are based on industry best practices and feedback from stakeholders, and provide recommendations for developing policies and procedures to eliminate or reduce workplace violence in a range of healthcare and social service settings.

These guidelines reflect the variations that exist in different settings and incorporate the latest and most effective ways to reduce the risk of violence in the workplace. Workplace setting determines not only the types of hazards that exist, but also the measures that will be available and appropriate to reduce or eliminate workplace violence hazards.

For the purpose of these guidelines, we have identified five different settings:

- **Hospital** settings represent large institutional medical facilities;
- **Residential Treatment** settings include institutional facilities such as nursing homes, and other long-term care facilities;
- **Non-residential Treatment/Service** settings include small neighborhood clinics and mental health centers;
- **Community Care** settings include community-based residential facilities and group homes; and
- **Field work** settings include home healthcare workers or social workers who make home visits.

Indeed, these guidelines are intended to cover a broad spectrum of workers, including those in: psychiatric facilities, hospital emergency departments, community mental health clinics, drug abuse treatment centers, pharmacies, community-care centers, and long-term care facilities. Healthcare and social service workers covered by these guidelines include: registered nurses, nurses' aides, therapists, technicians, home healthcare workers, social workers, emergency medical care personnel, physicians, pharmacists, physicians' assistants, nurse practitioners, and other support staff who come in contact with clients with known histories of violence. Employers should use these guidelines to develop appropriate workplace violence prevention programs, engaging workers to ensure their perspective is recognized and their needs are incorporated into the program.

Violence in the Workplace: The Impact of Workplace Violence on Healthcare and Social Service Workers

Healthcare and social service workers face a significant risk of job-related violence. The National Institute for Occupational Safety and Health (NIOSH) defines workplace violence as "violent acts (including physical assaults and threats of assaults) directed toward persons at work or on duty."[1] According to the Bureau of Labor Statistics (BLS), 27 out of the 100 fatalities in healthcare and social service settings that occurred in 2013 were due to assaults and violent acts.

While media attention tends to focus on reports of workplace homicides, the vast majority of workplace violence incidents result in non-fatal, yet serious injuries. Statistics based on the Bureau of Labor Statistics (BLS) and National Crime Victimization Survey (NCVS)[2] data both reveal that workplace violence is a threat to those in the healthcare and social service settings. BLS data show that the majority of injuries from assaults at work that required days away from work occurred in the healthcare and social services settings. Between 2011 and 2013, workplace assaults ranged from 23,540 and 25,630 annually, with 70 to 74% occurring in healthcare and social service settings. For healthcare workers, assaults comprise 10-11% of workplace injuries involving days away from work, as compared to 3% of injuries of all private sector employees.

---

[1] CDC/NIOSH. Violence. Occupational Hazards in Hospitals. 2002.

[2] Cited in the U.S. Department of Justice, Office of Justice Programs, Bureau of Justice Statistics report, Workplace Violence, 1993-2009 National Crime Victimization Survey and the Census of Fatal Occupational Injuries. March 2011. (www.bjs.gov/content/pub/pdf/wv09.pdf)

In 2013, a large number of the assaults involving days away from work occurred at healthcare and social assistance facilities (ranging for 13 to 36 per 10,000 workers). By comparison, the days away from work due to violence for the private sector as a whole in 2013 were only approximately 3 per 10,000 full-time workers. The workplace violence rates highlighted in BLS data are corroborated by the NCVS, which estimates that between 1993 and 2009 healthcare workers had a 20% (6.5 per 1,000) overall higher rate of workplace violence than all other workers (5.1 per 1,000).[3] In addition, workplace violence in the medical occupations represented 10.2% of all workplace violence incidents. It should also be noted that research has found that workplace violence is underreported—suggesting that the actual rates may be much higher.

Risk Factors: Identifying and Assessing Workplace Violence Hazards

Healthcare and social service workers face an increased risk of work-related assaults resulting primarily from violent behavior of their patients, clients and/or residents. While no specific diagnosis or type of patient predicts future violence, epidemiological studies consistently demonstrate that inpatient and acute psychiatric services, geriatric long term care settings,

Healthcare workers
face significant risks of job-related violence
▼

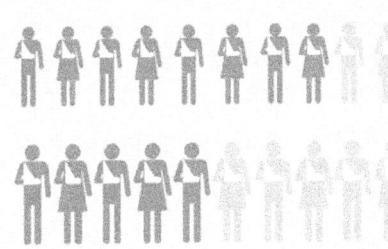

While under 20% of all workplace injuries happen to healthcare workers...

Healthcare workers suffer 50% of all assaults.

Source: Bureau of Labor Statistics

---

[3] The report defined medical occupations as: physicians, nurses, technicians, and other medical professionals.

high volume urban emergency departments and residential and day social services present the highest risks. Pain, devastating prognoses, unfamiliar surroundings, mind and mood altering medications and drugs, and disease progression can also cause agitation and violent behaviors.

While the individual risk factors will vary, depending on the type and location of a healthcare or social service setting, as well as the type of organization, some of the risk factors include:

Patient, Client and Setting-Related Risk Factors

- Working directly with people who have a history of violence, abuse drugs or alcohol, gang members, and relatives of patients or clients;

- Transporting patients and clients;

- Working alone in a facility or in patients' homes;

- Poor environmental design of the workplace that may block employees' vision or interfere with their escape from a violent incident;

- Poorly lit corridors, rooms, parking lots and other areas;[4]

- Lack of means of emergency communication;

- Prevalence of firearms, knives and other weapons among patients and their families and friends; and

- Working in neighborhoods with high crime rates.

Organizational Risk Factors

- Lack of facility policies and staff training for recognizing and managing escalating hostile and assaultive behaviors from patients, clients, visitors, or staff;

- Working when understaffed—especially during mealtimes and visiting hours;

- High worker turnover;

- Inadequate security and mental health personnel on site;

---

[4] CDC/NIOSH. Violence. Occupational Hazards in Hospitals. 2002.

- Long waits for patients or clients and overcrowded, uncomfortable waiting rooms;

- Unrestricted movement of the public in clinics and hospitals; and

- Perception that violence is tolerated and victims will not be able to report the incident to police and/or press charges.

Violence Prevention Programs

A written program for workplace violence prevention, incorporated into an organization's overall safety and health program, offers an effective approach to reduce or eliminate the risk of violence in the workplace. The building blocks for developing an effective workplace violence prevention program include:

(1) Management commitment and employee participation,

(2) Worksite analysis,

(3) Hazard prevention and control,

(4) Safety and health training, and

(5) Recordkeeping and program evaluation.

A violence prevention program focuses on developing processes and procedures appropriate for the workplace in question.

Specifically, a workplace's violence prevention program should have clear goals and objectives for preventing workplace violence, be suitable for the size and complexity of operations and be adaptable to specific situations and specific facilities or units. The components are interdependent and require regular reassessment and adjustment to respond to changes occurring within an organization, such as expanding a facility or changes in managers, clients, or procedures. And, as with any occupational safety and health program, it should be evaluated and reassessed on a regular basis. Those developing a workplace violence prevention program should also check for applicable state requirements. Several states have passed legislation and developed requirements that address workplace violence.

1. Management Commitment and Worker Participation

Management commitment and worker participation are essential elements of an effective violence prevention program. The leadership of management in providing full support for the development of the workplace's program, combined with worker involvement is critical for the success of the program. Developing procedures to ensure that management and employees are involved in the creation and operation of a workplace violence prevention program can be achieved through regular meetings— possibly as a team or committee.[5]

Effective management leadership begins by recognizing that workplace violence is a safety and health hazard.

Effective management leadership begins by recognizing that workplace violence is a safety and health hazard. Management commitment, including the endorsement and visible involvement of top management, provides the motivation and resources for workers and employers to deal effectively with workplace violence. This commitment should include:

- Acknowledging the value of a safe and healthful, violence-free workplace and ensuring and exhibiting equal commitment to the safety and health of workers and patients/clients;

- Allocating appropriate authority and resources to all responsible parties. Resource needs often go beyond financial needs to include access to information, personnel, time, training, tools, or equipment;

- Assigning responsibility and authority for the various aspects of the workplace violence prevention program to ensure that all managers and supervisors understand their obligations;

- Maintaining a system of accountability for involved managers, supervisors and workers;

- Supporting and implementing appropriate recommendations from safety and health committees;

---

[5] If employers take this approach, they should consult and follow the applicable provisions of the *National Labor Relations Act*—29 U.S.C. 151-169.

- Establishing a comprehensive program of medical and psychological counseling and debriefing for workers who have experienced or witnessed assaults and other violent incidents and ensuring that trauma-informed care is available; and

- Establishing policies that ensure the reporting, recording, and monitoring of incidents and near misses and that no reprisals are made against anyone who does so in good faith.

Additionally, management should: (1) articulate a policy and establish goals; (2) allocate sufficient resources; and (3) uphold program performance expectations.

Through involvement and feedback, workers can provide useful information to employers to design, implement and evaluate the program. In addition, workers with different functions and at various organizational levels bring a broad range of experience and skills to program design, implementation, and assessment. Mental health specialists have the ability to appropriately characterize disease characteristics but may need training and input from threat assessment professionals. Direct care workers, in emergency departments or mental health, may bring very different perspectives to committee work. The range of viewpoints and needs should be reflected in committee composition. This involvement should include:

- Participation in the development, implementation, evaluation, and modification of the workplace violence prevention program;

- Participation in safety and health committees that receive reports of violent incidents or security problems, making facility inspections and responding to recommendations for corrective strategies;

- Providing input on additions to or redesigns of facilities;

- Identifying the daily activities that employees believe put them most at risk for workplace violence;

- Discussions and assessments to improve policies and procedures—including complaint and suggestion programs designed to improve safety and security;

- Ensuring that there is a way to report and record incidents and near misses, and that issues are addressed appropriately;

- Ensuring that there are procedures to ensure that employees are not retaliated against for voicing concerns or reporting injuries; and

- Employee training and continuing education programs.

2. Worksite Analysis and Hazard Identification

A worksite analysis involves a mutual step-by-step assessment of the workplace to find existing or potential hazards that may lead to incidents of workplace violence. Cooperation between workers and employers in identifying and assessing hazards is the foundation of a successful violence prevention program. The assessment should be made by a team that includes senior management, supervisors and workers. Although management is responsible for controlling hazards, workers have a critical role to play in helping to identify and assess workplace hazards, because of their

Cooperation between workers and employers in identifying and assessing hazards is the foundation of a successful violence prevention program.

knowledge and familiarity with facility operations, process activities and potential threats. Depending on the size and structure of the organization, the team may also include representatives from operations; employee assistance; security; occupational safety and health; legal; and human resources staff. The assessment should include a records review, a review of the procedures and operations for different jobs, employee surveys and workplace security analysis.

Once the worksite analysis is complete, it should be used to identify the types of hazard prevention and control measures needed to reduce or eliminate the possibility of a workplace violence incident occurring. In addition, it should assist in the identification or development of appropriate training. The assessment team should also determine how often and under what circumstances worksite analyses should be conducted. For example, the team may determine that a comprehensive annual worksite analysis should be conducted, but require that an investigative analysis occur after every incident or near miss.

Additionally, those conducting the worksite analysis should periodically inspect the workplace and evaluate worker tasks in order to identify hazards, conditions, operations and situations that could lead to potential violence. The advice of independent reviewers, such as safety and health professionals, law enforcement or security specialists, and insurance safety auditors may be solicited to strengthen programs. These experts often provide a different perspective that serves to improve a program.

Information is generally collected through: (1) records analysis; (2) job hazard analysis; (3) employee surveys; and (4) patient/client surveys.

Records analysis and tracking

Records review is important to identify patterns of assaults or near misses that could be prevented or reduced through the implementation of appropriate controls. Records review should include medical, safety, specific threat assessments, workers' compensation and insurance records. The review should also include the OSHA Log of Work-Related Injuries and Illnesses (OSHA Form 300) if the employer is required to maintain one. In addition, incident/near-miss logs, a facility's general event or daily log and police reports should be reviewed to identify assaults relative to particular:

- Departments/Units;
- Work areas;
- Job titles;
- Activities—such as transporting patients between units or facilities, patient intake; and
- Time of day.

Possible Findings from Records Review:

	Hospital	Residential Treatment	Non-residential Treatment/ Service	Community Care	Field Workers (Home Healthcare and Social Service)
Departments/ Units	· Emergency Department · Psychiatric Unit · Geriatric Unit	· Dementia Unit · Adolescent Unit			
Work areas	· Waiting room · Nurses' station · Hallway · Treatment rooms	· Therapy room · Patient's room · Dining area · Van/Car transport	· Waiting area · Therapy room	· Kitchen · Car	· Kitchen · Car · Bedroom
Job titles	· Security guard · Nurse · Therapist · Doctor · Receptionist · Health aide · Technician	· Social worker · Therapist · Nurse · Health aide · Security guard · Driver · Technician	· Social worker · Behavioral health specialist · Nurse · Technician	· Social worker · Therapist · Health aide	· Social worker · Health aide · Child Support services · Emergency medical personnel
Activities	· Patient intake · Transferring patients from one floor to another · Meal time · Bathing · Changing of staff · Scanning for weapons	· Conducting therapy · Transitioning patients from one area to another · Driving patients · Feeding patient	· Therapy room · Client intake	· Conducting therapy · Bathing/ changing/ feeding client · Administering meds · Driving patient	· Bathing/ changing/ feeding client · Administering meds · Driving patient · Interacting with clients' families
Time of day	· After 10 PM · Meal times	· Late afternoon and evening	· No pattern	· Entry or exit	· Entry or exit · Meal times

Job Hazard Analysis

A job hazard analysis is an assessment that focuses on job tasks to identify hazards. Through review of procedures and operations connected to specific tasks or positions to identify if they contribute to hazards related to workplace violence and/or can be modified to reduce the likelihood of violence occurring, it examines the relationship between the employee, the task, tools, and the work environment. Worker participation is an essential component of the analysis. As noted in OSHA's publication on job hazard analyses,[6] priority should be given to specific types of job. For example, priority should be given to:

■ Jobs with high assault rates due to workplace violence;

■ Jobs that are new to an operation or have undergone procedural changes that may increase the potential for workplace violence; and

■ Jobs that require written instructions, such as procedures for administering medicine, and steps required for transferring patients.

After an incident or near miss, the analysis should focus on:

■ Analyzing those positions that were affected;

■ Identifying if existing procedures and operations were followed and if not, why not (in some instances, not following procedures could result in more effective protections);

■ Identifying if staff were adequately qualified and/or trained for the tasks required; and

■ Developing, if necessary, new procedures and operations to improve staff safety and security.

Employee surveys

Employee questionnaires or surveys are effective ways for employers to identify potential hazards that may lead to violent incidents, identify the types of problems workers face in their daily activities, and assess the effects of changes in

---

[6] OSHA 3071-2002 (Revised). *Job Hazard Analysis.*

work processes. Detailed baseline screening surveys can help pinpoint tasks that put workers at risk. Periodic surveys—conducted at least annually or whenever operations change or incidents of workplace violence occur—help identify new or previously unnoticed risk factors and deficiencies or failures in work practices. The periodic review process should also include feedback and follow-up. The following are sample questions:

- What daily activities, if any, expose you to the greatest risk of violence?

- What, if any, work activities make you feel unprepared to respond to a violent action?

- Can you recommend any changes or additions to the workplace violence prevention training you received?

- Can you describe how a change in a patient's daily routine affected the precautions you take to address the potential for workplace violence?

Client/Patient Surveys

Clients and patients may also have valuable feedback that may enable those being served by the facility to provide useful information to design, implement, and evaluate the program. Clients and patients may be able to participate in identifying triggers to violence, daily activities that may lead to violence, and effective responses.

3. Hazard Prevention and Control

After the systematic worksite analysis is complete, the employer should take the appropriate steps to prevent or control the hazards that were identified. To do this, the employer should: (1) identify and evaluate control options for workplace hazards; (2) select effective and feasible controls to eliminate or reduce hazards; (3) implement these controls in the workplace; (4) follow up to confirm that these controls are being used and maintained properly; and (5) evaluate the effectiveness of controls and improve, expand, or update them as needed.

In the field of industrial hygiene, these steps are generally categorized, in order of effectiveness, as (1) substitution; (2) engineering controls; and (3) administrative and work practice controls. These principles, which are described in more detail below, can also be applied to the field of workplace violence. In addition, employers should ensure that, if an incident of workplace violence occurs, post-incident procedures and services are in place and/or immediately made available.

Substitution

The best way to eliminate a hazard is to eliminate it or substitute a safer work practice. While these substitutions may be difficult in the therapeutic healthcare environment, an example may be transferring a client or patient to a more appropriate facility if the client has a history of violent behavior that may not be appropriate in a less secure therapeutic environment.

Engineering controls and workplace adaptations to minimize risk

Engineering controls are physical changes that either remove the hazard from the workplace or create a barrier between the worker and the hazard. In facilities where it is appropriate, there are several engineering control measures that can effectively prevent or control workplace hazards. Engineering control strategies include: (a) using physical barriers (such as enclosures or guards) or door locks to reduce employee exposure to the hazard; (b) metal detectors; (c) panic buttons, (d) better or additional lighting; and (e) more accessible exits (where appropriate). The measures taken should be site-specific and based on the hazards identified in the worksite analysis appropriate to the specific therapeutic setting. For example, closed circuit videos and bulletproof glass may be appropriate in a hospital or other institutional setting, but not in a community care facility. Similarly, it should be noted that services performed in the field (e.g., home health or social services) often occur in private residences where some engineering controls may not be possible or appropriate.

If new construction or modifications are planned for a facility, assess any plans to eliminate or reduce security hazards.

The following are possible engineering controls that could apply in different settings. Note that this is a list of suggested measures whose appropriateness will depend on a number of factors.

Possible engineering controls for different healthcare and social service settings

	Hospital	Residential Treatment	Non-residential Treatment/ Service	Community Care	Field Workers (Home Healthcare, Social Service)
Security/ silenced alarm systems	· Panic buttons or paging system at workstations or personal alarm devices worn by employees			· Paging system · GPS tracking[7] · Cell phones	
	· Security/silenced alarm systems should be regularly maintained and managers and staff should fully understand the range and limitations of the system.				
Exit routes	· Where possible, rooms should have two exits · Provide employee 'safe room' for emergencies · Arrange furniture so workers have a clear exit route		· Where possible, counseling rooms should have two exits · Arrange furniture so workers have a clear exit route	· Managers and workers should assess homes for exit routes	
	· Workers should be familiar with a site and identify the different exit routes available.				
Metal detectors – hand-held or installed	· Employers and workers will have to determine the appropriate balance of creating the suitable atmosphere for services being provided and the types of barriers put in place. · Metal detectors should be regularly maintained and assessed for effectiveness in reducing the weapons brought into a facility. · Staff should be appropriately assigned, and trained to use the equipment and remove weapons.				
Monitoring systems & natural surveillance	· Closed-circuit video – inside and outside · Curved mirrors · Proper placement of nurses' stations to allow visual scanning of areas · Glass panels in doors/walls for better monitoring		· Closed-circuit video – inside and outside · Curved mirrors · Glass panels in doors for better monitoring		
	· Employers and workers will have to determine the appropriate balance of creating the suitable atmosphere for services being provided and the types of barriers put in place. · Staff should know if video monitoring is in use or not and whether someone is always monitoring the video or not.				

---

[7] Employers and workers should determine the most effective method for ensuring the safety of workers without negatively impacting working conditions.

	Hospital	Residential Treatment	Non-residential Treatment/ Service	Community Care	Field Workers (Home Healthcare, Social Service)
Barrier protection	· Enclosed receptionist desk with bulletproof glass · Deep counters at nurses' stations · Lock doors to staff counseling and treatment rooms · Provide lockable (or keyless door systems) and secure bathrooms for staff members (with locks on the inside)— separated from patient/ client and visitor facilities · Lock all unused doors to limit access, in accord with local fire codes	· Deep counters in offices · Provide lockable (or keyless door systems) and secure bathrooms for staff members (with locks on the inside)— separated from patient/ client and visitor facilities · Lock all unused doors to limit access, in accord with local fire codes	· Deep counters · Provide lockable (or keyless door systems) and secure bathrooms for staff members (with locks on the inside)— separated from patient/client and visitor facilities		
	· Employers and workers will have to determine the appropriate balance of creating the suitable atmosphere for the services being provided and the types of barriers put in place.				

	Hospital	Residential Treatment	Non-residential Treatment/ Service	Community Care	Field Workers (Home Healthcare, Social Service)
Patient/client areas	· Establish areas for patients/ clients to de-escalate · Provide comfortable waiting areas to reduce stress · Divide waiting areas to limit the spreading of agitation among clients/ visitors	· Establish areas for patients/ clients to de-escalate · Provide comfortable waiting areas to reduce stress · Assess staff rotations in facilities where clients become agitated by unfamiliar staff	· Provide comfortable waiting areas to reduce stress	· Establish areas for patients/ clients to de-escalate	· Establish areas for patients/ clients to de-escalate
	· Employers and workers will have to determine the appropriate balance of creating the suitable atmosphere for the services being provided and the types of barriers put in place.				
Furniture, materials & maintenance	· Secure furniture and other items that could be used as weapons · Replace open hinges on doors with continuous hinges to reduce pinching hazards · Ensure cabinets and syringe drawers have working locks · Pad or replace sharp edged objects (such as metal table frames) · Consider changing or adding materials to reduce noise in certain areas · Recess any hand rails, drinking fountains and any other protrusions · Smooth down or cover any sharp surfaces			· When feasible, secure furniture or other items that could be used as weapons · Ensure cabinets and syringe drawers have working locks · Pad or replace sharp edged objects (such as metal table frames) · Ensure carrying equipment for medical equipment, medicines and valuables have working locks	· Ensure carrying equipment for medical equipment, medicines and valuables have working locks
	· Employers and workers will have to establish a balance between creating the appropriate atmosphere for the services being provided and securing furniture.				

	Hospital	Residential Treatment	Non-residential Treatment/ Service	Community Care	Field Workers (Home Healthcare, Social Service)
Lighting	· Install bright, effective lighting—both indoors and outdoors on the grounds, in parking areas and walkways			· Ensure lighting is adequate in both the indoor and outdoor areas	· Work with client to ensure lighting is adequate in both the indoor and outdoor areas
	· Ensure burned out lights are replaced immediately. · While lighting should be effective it should not be harsh or cause undue glare.				
Travel vehicles	· Ensure vehicles are properly maintained · Where appropriate, consider physical barrier between driver and patients			· Ensure vehicles are properly maintained	

Administrative and work practice controls

Administrative and work practice controls are appropriate when engineering controls are not feasible or not completely protective. These controls affect the way staff perform jobs or tasks. Changes in work practices and administrative procedures can help prevent violent incidents. As with engineering controls, the practices chosen to abate workplace violence should be appropriate to the type of site and in response to hazards identified.

In addition to the specific measures listed below, training for administrative and treatment staff should include therapeutic procedures that are sensitive to the cause and stimulus of violence. For example, research has shown that Trauma Informed Care is a treatment technique that has been successfully instituted in inpatient psychiatric units as a way to reduce patient violence, and the need for seclusion and restraint. As explained by the Substance Abuse and Mental Health Services Administration, trauma-informed services are based on an understanding of the vulnerabilities or triggers of trauma for survivors and can be more supportive than traditional service delivery approaches, thus avoiding re-traumatization.[8]

---

[8] Referenced on the Substance Abuse and Mental Health Services Administration's website on February 25, 2013 (www.samhsa.gov/nctic).

The following are possible administrative controls that could apply in different settings.

Possible administrative and work practice controls for different healthcare and social service settings

	Hospital	Residential Treatment	Non-residential Treatment/Service	Community Care	Field Workers (Home Healthcare, Social Service)
Workplace violence response policy	· Clearly state to patients, clients, visitors and workers that violence is not permitted and will not be tolerated. · Such a policy makes it clear to workers that assaults are not considered part of the job or acceptable behavior.				
Tracking workers[9]		Traveling workers should: · have specific log-in and log-out procedures · be required to contact the office after each visit and managers should have procedures to follow-up if workers fail to do so		Workers should: · have specific log-in and log-out procedures · be required to contact the office after each visit and managers should have procedures to follow-up if workers fail to do so · be given discretion as to whether or not they begin or continue a visit if they feel threatened or unsafe	
	· Log-in/log-out procedures should include: · the name and address of client visited; · the scheduled time and duration of visit; · a contact number; · a code word used to inform someone of an incident/threat; · worker's vehicle description and license plate number; · details of any travel plans with client; · contacting office/supervisor with any changes.				
Tracking clients with a known history of violence	· Supervise the movement of patients throughout the facility · Update staff in shift report about violent history or incident		· Update staff in shift report about violent history or incident		· Report all violent incidents to employer

---

[9] Massachusetts Department of Mental Health Task Force on Staff and Client Safety. (2011). Report of the Massachusetts Department of Mental Health Task Force on Staff and Client Safety.

	Hospital	Residential Treatment	Non-residential Treatment/Service	Community Care	Field Workers (Home Healthcare, Social Service)

	· Determine the behavioral history of new and transferred patients and clients to learn about any past violent or assaultive behaviors.
	   · Identify any event triggers for clients, such as certain dates or visitors.
	   · Identify the type of violence including severity, pattern and intended purpose.
	   · Information gained should be used to formulate individualized plans for early identification and prevention of future violence.
	 · Establish a system—such as chart tags, log books or verbal census reports—to identify patients and clients with a history of violence and identify triggers and the best responses and means of de-escalation.
	 · Ensure workers know and follow procedures for updates to patients' and clients' behavior.
	 · Ensure patient and client confidentiality is maintained.
	 · Update as needed.
	 · If stalking is suspected, consider varying check-in and check-out times for affected workers and plan different travel routes for those workers.				

Working alone or in secure areas	· Treat and interview aggressive or agitated clients in relatively open areas that still maintain privacy and confidentiality · Ensure workers are not alone when performing intimate physical examinations of patients · Advise staff to exercise extra care in elevators and stairwells · Provide staff members with security escorts to parking areas during evening/ late hours— Ensure these areas are well lit and highly visible	· Advise staff to exercise extra care in elevators, stairwells · Provide staff members with security escorts to parking areas during evening/ late hours. Ensure these areas are well lit and highly visible	· Ensure workers have means of communication—either cell phones of panic buttons · Develop policy to determine when a buddy system should be implemented	· Advise staff to exercise extra care in unfamiliar residences · Workers should be given discretion to receive backup assistance by another worker or law enforcement officer · Workers should be given discretion as to whether or not they begin or continue a visit if they feel threatened or unsafe · Ensure workers have means of communication—either cell phones or panic buttons
	· Limit workers from working alone in emergency areas or walk-in clinics, particularly at night or when assistance is unavailable. · Establish policies and procedures for secured areas and emergency evacuations. · Use the "buddy system," especially when personal safety may be threatened.				
Reporting	· Require workers to report all assaults or threats to a supervisor or manager (for example, through a confidential interview). Keep logbooks and reports of such incidents to help determine any necessary actions to prevent recurrences. · Establish a liaison with local police, service providers who can assist (e.g., counselors) and state prosecutors. When needed, give police physical layouts of facilities to expedite investigations.				

	Hospital	Residential Treatment	Non-residential Treatment/Service	Community Care	Field Workers (Home Healthcare, Social Service)
Entry procedures	· Provide responsive, timely information to those waiting; adopt measures to reduce waiting times · Institute sign-in procedures and visitor passes · Enforce visitor hours and procedures for being in the hospital · Have a "restricted visitors" list for patients with a history of violence/ gang activity; make copies available to security, nurses, and sign-in clerk	· Institute sign-in procedures with passes for visitors · Enforce visitor hours and procedures · Establish a list of "restricted visitors" for patients with a history of violence or gang activity; make copies available at security checkpoints, nurses' stations and visitor sign-in areas	· Provide responsive, timely information to those waiting; adopt measures to reduce waiting times	· Ensure workers determine how best to enter facilities	· Ensure workers determine how best to enter clients' homes
Incident response/ high risk activities	· Use properly trained security officers and counselors to respond to aggressive behavior; follow written security procedures · Ensure that adequate and qualified staff members are available at all times, especially during high-risk times such as patient transfers, emergency responses, mealtimes and at night · Ensure that adequate and qualified staff members are available to disarm and de-escalate patients if necessary · Assess changing client routines and activities to reduce or eliminate the possibility of violent outbursts		· Use properly trained security officers and counselors to respond to aggressive behavior; follow written security procedures		· Ensure assistance if children will be removed from the home

	Hospital	Residential Treatment	Non-residential Treatment/Service	Community Care	Field Workers (Home Healthcare, Social Service)
	• Advise workers of company procedures for requesting police assistance or filing charges when assaulted—and assist them in doing so if necessary. • Provide management support during emergencies. Respond promptly to all complaints. • Ensure that adequately trained staff members and counselors are available to de-escalate a situation and counsel patients. • Prepare contingency plans to treat clients who are "acting out" or making verbal or physical attacks or threats. • Emergency action plans should be developed to ensure that workers know how to call for help or medical assistance.				
Employee uniforms/ dress	• Provide staff with identification badges, preferably without last names, to readily verify employment. • Discourage workers from wearing necklaces or chains to help prevent possible strangulation in confrontational situations. • Discourage workers from wearing expensive jewelry or carrying large sums of money. • Discourage workers from carrying keys or other items that could be used as weapons. • Encourage the use of head netting/cap so hair cannot be grabbed and used to pull or shove workers.				
Facility & work procedures	• Survey facility periodically to remove tools or possessions left by visitors or staff that could be used inappropriately by patients • Survey facilities regularly to ensure doors that should be locked are locked—smoking policies should not allow these doors to be propped open • Keep desks and work areas free of items, including extra pens and pencils, glass photo frames, etc.	• Survey facility periodically to remove tools or possessions left by visitors or staff that could be used inappropriately by patients • Keep desks and work areas free of items, including extra pens and pencils, glass photo frames, etc.	• Survey facility periodically to remove tools or possessions left by visitors or staff that could be used inappropriately by patients • Establish daily work plans to keep a designated contact person informed about employees' whereabouts throughout the workday; have a contact person follow up if an employee does not report in as expected	• Have clear contracts on how home visits will be conducted, the presence of others in the home during visits and the refusal to provide services in clearly hazardous situations • Establish daily work plans to keep a designated contact person informed about employees' whereabouts throughout the workday; have a contact person follow up if an employee does not report in as expected	

	Hospital	Residential Treatment	Non-residential Treatment/Service	Community Care	Field Workers (Home Healthcare, Social Service)
Transportation procedures	· Develop safety procedures that specifically address the transport of patients. · Ensure that workers transporting patients have an effective and reliable means of communicating with their home office				· Develop safety procedures that specifically address the transport of patients. · Ensure that workers transporting patients have an effective and reliable means of communicating with their home office

Post-incident procedures and services

Post-incident response and evaluation are important components to an effective violence prevention program. Investigating incidents of workplace violence thoroughly will provide a roadmap to avoiding fatalities and injuries associated with future incidents. The purpose of the investigation should be to identify the "root cause" of the incident. Root causes, if not corrected, will inevitably recreate the conditions for another incident to occur.

When an incident occurs, the immediate first steps are to provide first aid and emergency care for the injured worker(s) and to take any measures necessary to prevent others from being injured. All workplace violence programs should provide comprehensive treatment for workers who are victimized personally or may be traumatized by witnessing a workplace violence incident. Injured staff should receive prompt treatment and psychological evaluation whenever an assault takes place, regardless of its severity—free of charge. Also, injured workers should be provided transportation to medical care if not available on site.

Victims of workplace violence could suffer a variety of consequences in addition to their actual physical injuries. These may include:

- Short- and long-term psychological trauma;
- Fear of returning to work;
- Changes in relationships with coworkers and family;
- Feelings of incompetence, guilt, powerlessness; and
- Fear of criticism by supervisors or managers.

Consequently, a strong follow-up program for these workers will not only help them address these problems but also help prepare them to confront or prevent future incidents of violence.

Several types of assistance can be incorporated into the post-incident response. For example, trauma-crisis counseling, critical-incident stress debriefing or employee assistance programs may be provided to assist victims. As explained by the Substance Abuse and Mental Health Services Administration, trauma-informed services are based on an understanding of the vulnerabilities or triggers of trauma for survivors and can be more supportive than traditional service delivery approaches, thus avoiding re-traumatization.[10] Whether the support is trauma-informed or not, certified employee assistance professionals, psychologists, psychiatrists, clinical nurse specialists or social workers should provide this counseling. Alternatively, the employer may refer staff victims to an outside specialist. In addition, the employer may establish an employee counseling service, peer counseling, or support groups.

Counselors should be well trained and have a good understanding of the issues and consequences of assaults and other aggressive, violent behavior. Appropriate and promptly rendered post-incident debriefings and counseling reduce acute psychological trauma and general stress levels among victims and witnesses. In addition, this type of counseling educates staff about workplace violence and positively influences workplace and organizational cultural norms to reduce trauma associated with future incidents.

Investigation of Incidents

Once these immediate needs are taken care of, the investigation should begin promptly. The basic steps in conducting incident investigations are:

1. *Report as required.* Determine who needs to be notified, both within the organization and outside (e.g., authorities), when there is an incident. Understand what types of

---

[10] Referenced on the Substance Abuse and Mental Health Services Administration's website on February 25, 2013 (www.samhsa.gov/nctic).

incidents must be reported, and what information needs to be included. If the incident involves hazardous materials additional reporting requirements may apply.

2. *Involve workers in the incident investigation.* The employees who work most closely in the area where the event occurred may have special insight into the causes and solutions.

3. *Identify Root Causes:* Identify the root causes of the incident. Don't stop an investigation at "worker error" or "unpredictable event." Ask "why" the patient or client acted, "why" the worker responded in a certain way, etc.

4. *Collect and review other information.* Depending on the nature of the incident, records related to training, maintenance, inspections, audits, and past incident reports may be relevant to review.

Identify the root causes of the incident. Don't stop an investigation at "worker error" or "unpredictable event." Ask "why" the patient or client acted, "why" the worker responded in a certain way, etc.

5. *Investigate Near Misses.* In addition to investigating all incidents resulting in a fatality, injury or illness, any near miss (a situation that could potentially have resulted in death, injury, or illness) should be promptly investigated as well. Near misses are caused by the same conditions that produce more serious outcomes, and signal that some hazards are not being adequately controlled, or that previously unidentified hazards exist.

4. Safety and Health Training

Education and training are key elements of a workplace violence protection program, and help ensure that all staff members are aware of potential hazards and how to protect themselves and their coworkers through established policies and procedures. Such training can be part of a broader type of instruction that includes protecting patients and clients (such as training on de-escalation techniques). However, employers should ensure that worker safety is a separate component that is thoroughly addressed.

Training for all workers

Training can: (1) help raise the overall safety and health knowledge across the workforce, (2) provide employees with the tools needed to identify workplace safety and security hazards, and (3) address potential problems before they arise and ultimately reduce the likelihood of workers being assaulted. The training program should involve all workers, including contract workers, supervisors, and managers. Workers who may face safety and security hazards should receive formal instruction on any specific or potential hazards associated with the unit or job and the facility. Such training may include information on the types of injuries or problems identified in the facility and the methods to control the specific hazards. It may also include instructions to limit physical interventions in workplace altercations whenever possible.

Every worker should understand the concept of "universal precautions for violence"— that is, that violence should be expected but can be avoided or mitigated through preparation. In addition, workers should understand the importance of a culture of respect, dignity, and active mutual engagement in preventing workplace violence.

New and reassigned workers should receive an initial orientation before being assigned their job duties. All workers should receive required training annually. In high-risk settings and institutions, refresher training may be needed more frequently, perhaps monthly or quarterly, to effectively reach and inform all workers. Visiting staff, such as physicians, should receive the same training as permanent staff and contract workers. Qualified trainers should instruct at the comprehension level appropriate for the staff. Effective training programs should involve role-playing, simulations and drills.

Training topics

Training topics may include management of assaultive behavior, professional/police assault-response training, or personal safety training on how to prevent and avoid assaults.

A combination of training programs may be used, depending on the severity of the risk.

In general, training should cover the policies and procedures for a facility as well as de-escalation and self-defense techniques. Both de-escalation and self-defense training should include a hands-on component. The following provides a list of possible topics:

- The workplace violence prevention policy;

- Risk factors that cause or contribute to assaults;

- Policies and procedures for documenting patients' or clients' change in behavior;

- The location, operation, and coverage of safety devices such as alarm systems, along with the required maintenance schedules and procedures;

- Early recognition of escalating behavior or recognition of warning signs or situations that may lead to assaults;

- Ways to recognize, prevent or diffuse volatile situations or aggressive behavior, manage anger and appropriately use medications;

- Ways to deal with hostile people other than patients and clients, such as relatives and visitors;

- Proper use of safe rooms—areas where staff can find shelter from a violent incident;

- A standard response action plan for violent situations, including the availability of assistance, response to alarm systems and communication procedures;

- Self-defense procedures where appropriate;

- Progressive behavior control methods and when and how to apply restraints properly and safety when necessary;

- Ways to protect oneself and coworkers, including use of the "buddy system";

- Policies and procedures for reporting and recordkeeping;

- Policies and procedures for obtaining medical care, trauma-informed care, counseling, workers' compensation or legal assistance after a violent episode or injury.

Training for supervisors and managers

Supervisors and managers must be trained to recognize high-risk situations, so they can ensure that workers are not placed in assignments that compromise their safety. Such training should include encouraging workers to report incidents and to seek the appropriate care after experiencing a violent incident.

Supervisors and managers must be trained to recognize high-risk situations, so they can ensure that workers are not placed in assignments that compromise their safety.

Supervisors and managers should learn how to reduce safety hazards and ensure that workers receive appropriate training. Following training, supervisors and managers should be able to recognize a potentially hazardous situation and make any necessary changes in the physical plant, patient care treatment program and staffing policy, and procedures to reduce or eliminate the hazards.

Training for security personnel

Security personnel need specific training from the hospital or clinic, including the psychological components of handling aggressive and abusive clients, and ways to handle aggression and defuse hostile situations.

Evaluation of training

The training program should also include an evaluation. At least annually, the team or coordinator responsible for the program should review its content, methods and the frequency of training. Program evaluation may involve supervisor and employee interviews, testing, observing and reviewing reports of behavior of individuals in threatening situations.

5. Recordkeeping and Program Evaluation

Recordkeeping and evaluation of the violence prevention program are necessary to determine its overall effectiveness and identify any deficiencies or changes that should be made.

Accurate records of injuries, illnesses, incidents, assaults, hazards, corrective actions, patient histories and training can help employers determine the severity of the problem; identify any developing trends or patterns in particular locations, jobs or departments; evaluate methods of hazard control; identify training needs and develop solutions for an effective program. Records can be especially useful to large organizations and for members of a trade association that "pool" data. Key records include:

- *OSHA Log of Work-Related Injuries and Illnesses (OSHA Form 300).* Covered employers are required to prepare and maintain records of serious occupational injuries and illnesses, using the OSHA 300 Log. As of January 2015, all employers must report: (1) all work-related fatalities within 8 hours and (2) all work-related inpatient hospitalizations, all amputations and all losses of an eye within 24 hours. Injuries caused by assaults must be entered on the log if they meet the recording criteria.[11]

- *Medical reports of work injury, workers' compensation reports and supervisors' reports for each recorded assault.* These records should describe the type of assault, such as an unprovoked sudden attack or patient-to-patient altercation, who was assaulted, and all other circumstances of the incident. The records should include a description of the environment or location, lost work time that resulted and the nature of injuries sustained. These medical records are confidential documents and should be kept in a locked location under the direct responsibility of a healthcare professional.

- *Records of incidents of abuse, reports conducted by security personnel, verbal attacks or aggressive behavior that may be threatening,* such as pushing or shouting and acts of aggression toward other clients. This may be kept as part of an assaultive incident report. Ensure that the affected department evaluates these records routinely.

- *Information on patients with a history of past violence, drug abuse or criminal activity recorded on the patient's chart.* Anyone who cares for a potentially aggressive, abusive or

---

[11] 29 CFR Part 1904, revised 2014.

violent client should be aware of the person's background and history, including triggers and de-escalation responses. Log the admission of violent patients to help determine potential risks. Log violent events on patients' charts and flagged charts.[12]

▣ *Documentation of minutes of safety meetings, records of hazard analyses and corrective actions recommended and taken.*

▣ *Records of all training programs, attendees, and qualifications of trainers.*

Elements of a program evaluation

As part of their overall program, employers should evaluate their safety and security measures. Top management should review the program regularly and, with each incident, to evaluate its success. Responsible parties (including managers, supervisors and employees) should reevaluate policies and procedures on a regular basis to identify deficiencies and take corrective action.

Management should share workplace violence prevention evaluation reports with all workers. Any changes in the program should be discussed at regular meetings of the safety committee, union representatives or other employee groups.

All reports should protect worker and patient confidentiality either by presenting only aggregate data or by removing personal identifiers if individual data are used.

Processes involved in an evaluation include:

▣ Establishing a uniform violence reporting system and regular review of reports;

▣ Reviewing reports and minutes from staff meetings on safety and security issues;

▣ Analyzing trends and rates in illnesses, injuries or fatalities caused by violence relative to initial or "baseline" rates;

▣ Measuring improvement based on lowering the frequency and severity of workplace violence;

---

[12] Proper patient confidentiality must be maintained.

- Keeping up-to-date records of administrative and work practice changes to prevent workplace violence to evaluate how well they work;

- Surveying workers before and after making job or worksite changes or installing security measures or new systems to determine their effectiveness;

- Tracking recommendations through to completion;

- Keeping abreast of new strategies available to prevent and respond to violence in the healthcare and social service fields as they develop;

- Surveying workers periodically to learn if they experience hostile situations in performing their jobs;

- Complying with OSHA and state requirements for recording and reporting injuries, illnesses, and fatalities; and

- Requesting periodic law enforcement or outside consultant review of the worksite for recommendations on improving worker safety.

Workplace Violence Program Checklists

These checklists can help you or your workplace violence/crime prevention committee evaluate the workplace and job tasks to identify situations that may place workers at risk of assault. It is not designed for a specific industry or occupation, and may be used for any workplace. Adapt the checklist to fit your own needs. It is very comprehensive and not every question will apply to your workplace—if the question does not apply, either delete or write "N/A" in the NOTES column. Add any other questions that may be relevant to your worksite.

1. RISK FACTORS FOR WORKPLACE VIOLENCE

Cal/OSHA and NIOSH have identified the following risk factors that may contribute to violence in the workplace. If you have one or more of these risk factors in your workplace, there may be a potential for violence.

	YES	NO	Notes/Follow-up Action
Do employees have contact with the public?			
Do they exchange money with the public?			
Do they work alone?			
Do they work late at night or during early morning hours?			
Is the workplace often understaffed?			
Is the workplace located in an area with a high crime rate?			
Do employees enter areas with a high crime rate?			
Do they have a mobile workplace (patrol vehicle, work van, etc.)?			
Do they deliver passengers or goods?			
Do employees perform jobs that might put them in conflict with others?			
Do they ever perform duties that could upset people (deny benefits, confiscate property, terminate child custody, etc.)?			
Do they deal with people known or suspected of having a history of violence?			
Do any employees or supervisors have a history of assault, verbal abuse, harassment, or other threatening behavior?			
Other risk factors – please describe:			

2. INSPECTING WORK AREAS

■ Who is responsible for building security?_____

_____

■ Are workers told or can they identify who is responsible for security? Yes No

You or your workplace violence/crime prevention committee should now begin a "walkaround" inspection to identify potential security hazards. This inspection can tell you which hazards are already well controlled, and what control measures need to be added. Not all of the following questions may be answered through simple observation. You may also need to talk to workers or investigate in other ways.

	All Areas	Some Areas	Few Areas	No Areas	NOTES/FOLLOW-UP ACTION
Are nametags or ID cards required for employees (omitting personal information such as last name and home address)?					
Are workers notified of past violent acts in the workplace?					
Are trained security and counseling personnel accessible to workers in a timely manner?					
Do security and counseling personnel have sufficient authority to take all necessary action to ensure worker safety?					
Is there an established liaison with state police and/or local police and counseling agencies?					
Are bullet-resistant windows or similar barriers used when money is exchanged with the public?					
Are areas where money is exchanged visible to others who could help in an emergency? (For example, can you see cash register areas from outside?)					
Is a limited amount of cash kept on hand, with appropriate signs posted?					
Could someone hear a worker who calls for help?					
Can employees observe patients or clients in waiting areas?					
Do areas used for patient or client interviews allow co-workers to observe any problems?					
Are waiting areas and work areas free of objects that could be used as weapons?					
Are chairs and furniture secured to prevent their use as weapons?					
Is furniture in waiting areas and work areas arranged to prevent entrapment of workers?					
Are patient or client waiting areas designed to maximize comfort and minimize stress?					

	All Areas	Some Areas	Few Areas	No Areas	NOTES/FOLLOW-UP ACTION
Are patients or clients in waiting areas clearly informed how to use the department's services so they will not become frustrated?					
Are waiting times for patient or client services kept short to prevent frustration?					
Are private, locked restrooms available for employees?					
Is there a secure place for workers to store personal belongings?					

3. INSPECTING EXTERIOR BUILDING AREAS

	Yes	No	NOTES/FOLLOW-UP ACTION
Do workers feel safe walking to and from the workplace?			
Are the entrances to the building clearly visible from the street?			
Is the area surrounding the building free of bushes or other hiding places?			
Is lighting bright and effective in outside areas?			
Are security personnel provided outside the building?			
Is video surveillance provided outside the building?			
Are remote areas secured during off shifts?			
Is a buddy escort system required to remote areas during off shifts?			
Are all exterior walkways visible to security personnel?			

4. INSPECTING PARKING AREAS

	Yes	No	NOTES/FOLLOW-UP ACTION
Is there a nearby parking lot reserved for employees only?			
Is the parking lot attended or otherwise secured?			
Is the parking lot free of blind spots and is landscaping trimmed back to prevent hiding places?			
Is there enough lighting to see clearly in the parking lot and when walking to the building?			
Are security escorts available to employees walking to and from the parking lot?			

5. SECURITY MEASURES

Does the workplace have:	In Place	Should Add	Doesn't Apply	NOTES/FOLLOW-UP ACTION
Physical barriers (plexiglass partitions, bullet-resistant customer window, etc.)?				
Security cameras or closed-circuit TV in high-risk areas?				
Panic buttons?				
Alarm systems?				
Metal detectors?				
Security screening device?				
Door locks?				
Internal telephone system to contact emergency assistance?				
Telephones with an outside line programmed for 911?				
Two-way radios, pagers, or cellular telephones?				
Security mirrors (e.g., convex mirrors)?				
Secured entry (e.g., "buzzers")?				
Personal alarm devices?				
"Drop safes" to limit the amount of cash on hand?				
Broken windows repaired promptly?				
Security systems, locks, etc. tested on a regular basis and repaired promptly when necessary?				

6. COMMENTS

_____

_____

_____

_____

Checklist completed by: _____ Date: _____

Department/Location: _____

Phone Number: _____

Workplace Violence Prevention Program Assessment Checklist

Use this checklist as part of a regular safety and health inspection or audit to be conducted by the Health and Safety, Crime/Workplace Violence Prevention Coordinator, or joint labor/management committee. If a question does not apply to the workplace, then write "N/A" (not applicable) in the notes column. Add any other questions that may be appropriate.

	Yes	No	NOTES
STAFFING			
Is there someone responsible for building security?			
Who is it?			
Are workers told who is responsible for security?			
Is adequate and trained staffing available to protect workers who are in potentially dangerous situations?			
Are there trained security personnel accessible to workers in a timely manner?			
Do security personnel have sufficient authority to take all necessary action to ensure worker safety?			
Are security personnel provided outside the building?			
Is the parking lot attended or otherwise secure?			
Are security escorts available to walk employees to and from the parking lot?			

	Yes	No	NOTES
TRAINING			
Are workers trained in the emergency response plan (for example, escape routes, notifying the proper authorities)?			
Are workers trained to report violent incidents or threats?			
Are workers trained in how to handle difficult clients or patients?			
Are workers trained in ways to prevent or defuse potentially violent situations?			
Are workers trained in personal safety and self-defense?			
FACILITY DESIGN			
Are there enough exits and adequate routes of escape?			
Can exit doors be opened only from the inside to prevent unauthorized entry?			
Is the lighting adequate to see clearly in indoor areas?			
Are there employee-only work areas that are separate from public areas?			
Is access to work areas only through a reception area?			
Are reception and work areas designed to prevent unauthorized entry?			
Could someone hear a worker call for help?			
Can workers observe patients or clients in waiting areas?			
Do areas used for patient or client interviews allow co-workers to observe any problems?			
Are waiting and work areas free of objects that could be used as weapons?			
Are chairs and furniture secured to prevent their use as weapons?			
Is furniture in waiting and work areas arranged to prevent workers from becoming trapped?			
Are patient or client areas designed to maximize comfort and minimize stress?			
Is a secure place available for workers to store their personal belongings?			
Are private, locked restrooms available for staff?			

	Yes	No	NOTES
SECURITY MEASURES – **Does the workplace have?**			
Physical barriers (Plexiglas partitions, elevated counters to prevent people from jumping over them, bullet-resistant customer windows, etc.)?			
Security cameras or closed-circuit TV in high-risk areas?			
Panic buttons – (portable or fixed)			
Alarm systems?			
Metal detectors?			
X-ray machines?			
Door locks?			
Internal phone system to activate emergency assistance?			
Phones with an outside line programmed to call 911?			
Security mirrors (convex mirrors)?			
Secured entry (buzzers)?			
Personal alarm devices?			
OUTSIDE THE FACILITY			
Do workers feel safe walking to and from the workplace?			
Are the entrances to the building clearly visible from the street?			
Is the area surrounding the building free of bushes or other hiding places?			
Is video surveillance provided outside the building?			
Is there enough lighting to see clearly outside the building?			
Are all exterior walkways visible to security personnel?			
Is there a nearby parking lot reserved for employees only?			
Is the parking lot free of bushes or other hiding places?			
Is there enough lighting to see clearly in the parking lot and when walking to the building?			
Have neighboring facilities and businesses experienced violence or crime?			

	Yes	No	NOTES
WORKPLACE PROCEDURES			
Are employees given maps and clear directions in order to navigate the areas where they will be working?			
Is public access to the building controlled?			
Are floor plans posted showing building entrances, exits, and location of security personnel?			
Are these floor plans visible only to staff and not to outsiders?			
Is other emergency information posted, such as the telephone numbers?			
Are special security measures taken to protect people who work late at night (escorts, locked entrances, etc.)?			
Are visitors or clients escorted to offices for appointments?			
Are authorized visitors to the building required to wear ID badges?			
Are identification tags required for staff (omitting personal information such as the person's last name and social security number)?			
Are workers notified of past violent acts by particular clients, patients, etc.?			
Is there an established liaison with local police and counseling agencies?			
Are patients or clients in waiting areas clearly informed how to use the department's services so they will not become frustrated?			
Are waiting times for patient or client services kept short to prevent frustration?			
Are broken windows and locks repaired promptly?			
Are security devices (locks, cameras, alarms, etc.) tested on a regular basis and repaired promptly when necessary?			
FIELD WORK – Staffing:			
Are escorts or "buddies" provided for people who work in potentially dangerous situations?			
Is assistance provided to workers in the field in a timely manner when requested?			
FIELD WORK – Training:			
Are workers briefed about the area in which they will be working (gang colors, neighborhood culture, language, drug activity, etc.)?			

	Yes	No	NOTES
Can workers effectively communicate with people they meet in the field (same language, etc.)?			
Are people who work in the field late at night or early mornings advised about special precautions to take?			
FIELD WORK – Work Environment:			
Is there enough lighting to see clearly in all areas where workers must go?			
Are there safe places for workers to eat, use the restroom, store valuables, etc.?			
Are there places where workers can go for protection in an emergency?			
Is safe parking readily available for employees in the field?			
FIELD WORK – Security Measures:			
Are workers provided two-way radios, pagers, or cellular phones?			
Are workers provided with personal alarm devices or portable panic buttons?			
Are vehicle door and window locks controlled by the driver?			
Are vehicles equipped with physical barriers (Plexiglas partitions, etc.)?			
FIELD WORK – Work Procedures:			
Are employees given maps and clear directions for covering the areas where they will be working?			
Are employees given alternative routes to use in neighborhoods with a high crime rate?			
Does a policy exist to allow employees to refuse service to clients or customers (in the home, etc.) in a hazardous situation?			
Has a liaison with the police been established?			
Do workers avoid carrying unnecessary items that someone could use as weapon against them?			
Does the employer provide a safe vehicle or other transportation for use in the field?			
Are vehicles used in the field routinely inspected and kept in good working order?			
Is there always someone who knows where each employee is?			
Are nametags required for workers in the field (omitting personal information such as last name and social security number)?			
Are workers notified of past violent acts by particular clients, patients, etc.?			

	Yes	No	NOTES
FIELD WORK – Are special precautions taken when workers:			
Have to take something away from people (remove children from the home)?			
Have contact with people who behave violently?			
Use vehicles or wear clothing marked with the name of an organization that the public may strongly dislike?			
Perform duties inside people's homes?			
Have contact with dangerous animals (dogs, etc.)?			

Adapted from the workplace violence prevention program checklist, California Department of Human Resources, see www.calhr.ca.gov/Documents/model-workplace-violence-and-bullying-prevention-program.pdf (last accessed November 25, 2014).

Bibliography

Center for Disease Control. (2002). *Violence: Occupational Hazards in Hospitals.* Cincinnati: National Institute of Occupational Safety and Health.

Chapman, R., Perry, L., Styles, I., & Combs, S. (2009). Predicting patient agression against nurses in all hospital areas. *British Journal of Nursing*, 476-483.

Dillon, B. L. (2012). Workplace violence: Impact, causes, and prevention. *Work*, 15-20.

Duxbury, J., & Whittington, R. (2005). Causes and management of patient aggression and violence: staff and patient perspectives. *Journal of Advanced Nursing*, 469-478.

ECRI Institue. (2011). *Healthcare Risk Control: Violence in Healthcare Facilities.* Plymouth Meeting: ECRI Institute.

Erdmann, S. L. (2008-2009). Eat the Carrot and Use the Stick: the Prevalence of Workplace Violence Demands Proactive Federal Regulation of Employers. *Valparaiso University Law Review*, 725-770.

Farkas, G. M., & Tsukayama, J. K. (2012). An integrative approach to threat assessment and management: Security and mental health response to a threatening client. *Work*, 9-14.

Ferns, T., & Cork, A. (2008). Managing alcohol related aggression in the emergency department (Part I). *International Emergency Nursing*, 43-47.

Foley, M. (2012). Evaluating progress in reducing workplace violence: Trends in Washington State workers' compensation claims rates, 1997-2007. *Work*, 67-81.

Forster, J. A., Petty, M. T., Schleiger, C., & Walters, H. C. (2005). kNOw workplace violence: developing programs for managing the risk of aggression in the health care setting. *Medical Journal of Australia*, 357-361.

Gallant-Roman, M. A. (2008). Strategies and Tools to Reduce Workplace Violence. *American Association of Occupational Health Nurses* , 449-454.

Gates, D., Fitzwater, E., Telintelo, S., Succop, P., & Sommers, M. (2004). Preventing Assaults by Nursing Home Residents: Nursing Assistants' Knowledge and Confidence--A Pilot Study. *Journal of American Medical Directors Association*, S16-S21.

Geiger-Brown, J., Muntaner, C., McPhaul, K., Libscomb, J., & Trinkoff, A. http://laborcenter.berkeley.edu/homecare/pdf/geiger. pdf. Retrieved September 14, 2012, from http://laborcenter. berkeley.edu.

Gerson, R. R., Pogorzelska, M., Qureshi, K. A., Stone, P. W., Canton, A. N., Samar, S. M., et al. http://www.ahrq.gov/ downloads/pub/advances2/vol1/Advances-Gershon_88.pdf. Retrieved September 14, 2012, from www.ahrq.gov.

Gillespie, G. L., Gates, D. M., Miller, M., & Howard, P. K. (2010). Workplace Violence in Healthcare Settings: Risk Factors and Protective Strategies. *Rehabilitation Nursing*, 177-184.

Gillespie, G. L., Gates, D. M., Miller, M., & Howard, P. K. (2012). Emergency department workers' perceptions of security officers' effectiveness during violent events. *Work*, 21-27.

Greenspan, A. I., & Noonan, R. K. (2012). Twenty years of scientific progress in injury and violence research and the next public health frontier. *Journal of Safety Research*, Article in Press.

Harthill, S. (2009-2010). The Need for a Revitalized Regulatory Scheme to Address Workplace Bullying in the United States: Harnessing the Federal Occupational Safety and Health Act. *University of Cincinnati Law Review*, 1250-1306.

Hartley, D., Doman, B., Hendricks, S. A., & Jenkins, E. L. (2012). Non-fatal workplace violence injuries in the United States 2003-2004: A follow back study. *Work*, 125-135.

Ho, J. D., Clinton, J. E., Lappe, M. A., Heegaard, W. G., Williams, M. F., & Miner, J. R. (2011). Violence: Recognition, Management and Prevention: Introduction of the conducted electrical weapon into hospital setting. *The Journal of Emergency Medicine*, 317-323.

Hutchings, D., Lundrigan, E., Mathews, M., Lynch, A., & Goosney, J. (2010). Keeping Community Health Care Workers Safe. *Home Health Care Management Practice OnlineFirst*.

International Association for Healthcare Security & Safety (IAHSS). (2012). *IAHSS Handbook: Healthcare Security Basic Industry Guidelines*. Glendale Heights: IAHSS.

International Association for Healthcare Security & Safety. (2012). *Security Design Guidelines for Healthcare Facilities*. Glendale Heights: IAHSS.

Jenkins, E. L., Fisher, B. S., & Hartley, D. (2012). Safe and secure at work?: Findings from 2002 Workplace Risk Supplement. *Work*, 57-66.

Johns, D. V. (2008-2009). Action Should Follow Words: Assessing the Arbitral Response to Zero-Tolerance Workplace Violence Policies. *Ohio State Journal on Dispute Resolution*, 263-290.

Joint Programme on Workplace Violence in the Health Sector; International Labour Office (ILO); International Council of Nurses (IC); World Health Organization (WHO); Public Services International (PSI). (2002). *Framework Guidelines for Addressing Workplace Violence in the Health Sector.* Geneva: International Labour Office.

Kelen, G. D., & Catlett, C. L. (2010). Violence in the Health Care Setting. *The Journal of the American Medical Association*, 2530-2531.

Kowalenko, T., Cunningham, R., Sachs, C. J., Gore, R., Barata, I. A., Gates, D., et al. (2012). Violence: Recognition, Management and Prevention - Workplace Violence in Emergency Medicine: Current Knowledge and Future Directions. *The Journal of Emergency Medicine*, 523-531.

La, M. I., & Loomis, D. P. (2007). Frequency and determinants of recommended workplace violence prevention measures. *Journal of Safety Research*, 643-650.

Laden, V. A., & Schwartz, G. (2000). Psychiatric Disabilities, the Americans with Disabilities Act, and the New Workplace Violence Account. *Berkeley Journal of Employment and Labor Law*, 246-270.

Lipscomb, J. A., London, M., Chen, Y., Flannery, K., Watt, M. G.-B., Johnson, J., et al. (2012). Safety climate and workplace violence prevention in state-run residential addiction treatment centers. *Work*, 47-56.

Lipscomb, J., McPhaul, K., Rosen, J., Brown, J. G., Choi, M., Soeken, K., et al. (2006). Violence Prevention in the Mental Health Setting: The New York State Experience. *Canadian Journal of Nursing Research*, 96-117.

Lipscomb, J., Silverstein, B., Slavin, T. J., Cody, E., & Jenkins, L. (2002). Perspectives on Legal Strategies to Prevent Workplace Violence. *The Journal of Law, Medicine, & Ethics*, 166-172.

Magnavita, N. (2011). Violence Prevention in a Small-scale Psychiatric Unit: Program Planning and Evaluation. *International Journal of Occupational Environmental Health*, 336-344.

Massachusetts Department of Mental Health Task Force on Staff and Client Safety. (2011). *Report of the Massachusetts Department of Mental Health Task Force on Staff and Client Safety.*

McPaul, K., Libscomb, J., & Johnson, J. (2010). Assessing Risk for Violence on Home Health Visits. *Home Healthcare Nurse*, 278-289.

McPhaul, K. M., London, M., Murrett, K., Flannery, K., Rosen, J., & Lipscomb, J. (2008). Environmental Evaluation for Workplace Violence in Healthcare and Social Services. *Journal of Safety Research, 39*, 237-250.

Medley, D. B., Morris, J. E., Stone, C. K., Song, J., Delmas, T., & Thakrar, K. (2012). Administration of Emergency Medicine: An association between occupancy rates in the emergency department and rates of violence toward staff. *The Journal of Emergency Medicine*, 1-9.

Nachreiner, N. M., Hansen, H. E., Okano, A., Gerberich, S. G., Ryan, A. D., McGovern, P. M., et al. (2007). Difference in Work-Related Violence by Nurse License Type. *Journal of Professional Nursing*, 290-300.

NIOSH Fast Facts: Home Healthcare Workers - How to Prevent Violence on the Job. (2012, February). NIOSH.

Ontario Safety Association for Community & Healthcare. (2003). *Health & Safety in the Home Care Environment, Second Addition.* Toronto: Ontario Safety Association for Community & Healthcare.

Phillips, S. (2007). Countering Workplace Aggression: An Urban Tertiary Care Institutional Exemplar. *Nursing Administration Quarterly*, 209-218.

Rodriguez-Acosta, R., Myers, D., Richardson, D., Lipscomb, H., Chen, J., & Dement, J. (2010). Physical assault among nursing staff employed in acute care. *Work*, 191-200.

Sawyer, J. R. (2009). Preventing hospital gun violence: best practices for security professionals to review and adopt. *Journal of Healthcare Protection Management*, 99-103.

Smith, T. J. (2012). Active life-threatenting violence--are you prepared. *Journal of Healthcare Protection Management*, 28(1), 44-49.

Tak, S., Sweeney, M. H., Alterman, T. B., & Calvert, G. M. (2010). Workplace Assaults on Nursing Assistants in U.S. Nursing Homes: A Multilevel Analysis. *American Journal of Public Health*, 1938-45.

The Joint Commission. (2010, June 03). Sentinel Event Alert: Preventing violence in the health care setting. *(45)*. The Joint Commission.

Wiskow, C. (2003). *Guidelines on Workplace Violence in the Health Sector - Comparison of major known national guidelines and strategies: United Kingdom, Australia, Sweden, USA (OSHA and California)*. Geneva: ILO/ICN/WHO/PSI Joint Programme on Workplace Violence in the Health Sector.

Workers' Rights

Workers have the right to:

- Working conditions that do not pose a risk of serious harm.

- Receive information and training (in a language and vocabulary the worker understands) about workplace hazards, methods to prevent them, and the OSHA standards that apply to their workplace.

- Review records of work-related injuries and illnesses.

- File a complaint asking OSHA to inspect their workplace if they believe there is a serious hazard or that their employer is not following OSHA's rules. OSHA will keep all identities confidential.

- Exercise their rights under the law without retaliation, including reporting an injury or raising health and safety concerns with their employer or OSHA. If a worker has been retaliated against for using their rights, they must file a complaint with OSHA as soon as possible, but no later than 30 days.

For more information, see OSHA's Workers page.

OSHA Assistance, Services and Programs

OSHA has a great deal of information to assist employers in complying with their responsibilities under OSHA law. Several OSHA programs and services can help employers identify and correct job hazards, as well as improve their injury and illness prevention program.

Establishing an Injury and Illness Prevention Program

The key to a safe and healthful work environment is a comprehensive injury and illness prevention program.

Injury and illness prevention programs are systems that can substantially reduce the number and severity of workplace injuries and illnesses, while reducing costs to employers. Thousands of employers across the United States already manage safety using injury and illness prevention programs, and OSHA believes that all employers can and should do the same. Thirty-four states have requirements or voluntary guidelines for workplace injury and illness prevention programs. Most successful injury and illness prevention programs are based on a common set of key elements. These include management leadership, worker participation, hazard identification, hazard prevention and control, education and training, and program evaluation and improvement. Visit OSHA's Injury and Illness Prevention Programs web page at www.osha.gov/dsg/topics/safetyhealth for more information.

Compliance Assistance Specialists

OSHA has compliance assistance specialists throughout the nation located in most OSHA offices. Compliance assistance specialists can provide information to employers and workers about OSHA standards, short educational programs on specific hazards or OSHA rights and responsibilities, and information on additional compliance assistance resources. For more details, visit www.osha.gov/dcsp/compliance_assistance/cas.html or call 1-800-321-OSHA (6742) to contact your local OSHA office.

Free On-site Safety and Health Consultation Services for Small Business

OSHA's On-site Consultation Program offers free and confidential advice to small and medium-sized businesses in all states across the country, with priority given to high-hazard worksites. Each year, responding to requests from small employers looking to create or improve their safety and health management programs, OSHA's On-site Consultation Program conducts over 29,000 visits to small business worksites covering over 1.5 million workers across the nation.

On-site consultation services are separate from enforcement and do not result in penalties or citations. Consultants from state agencies or universities work with employers to identify workplace hazards, provide advice on compliance with OSHA standards, and assist in establishing safety and health management programs.

For more information, to find the local On-site Consultation office in your state, or to request a brochure on Consultation Services, visit www.osha.gov/consultation, or call 1-800-321-OSHA (6742).

Under the consultation program, certain exemplary employers may request participation in OSHA's **Safety and Health Achievement Recognition Program (SHARP)**. Eligibility for participation includes, but is not limited to, receiving a full-service, comprehensive consultation visit, correcting all identified hazards and developing an effective safety and health management program. Worksites that receive SHARP recognition are exempt from programmed inspections during the period that the SHARP certification is valid.

Cooperative Programs

OSHA offers cooperative programs under which businesses, labor groups and other organizations can work cooperatively with OSHA. To find out more about any of the following programs, visit www.osha.gov/cooperativeprograms.

Strategic Partnerships and Alliances

The OSHA Strategic Partnerships (OSP) provide the opportunity for OSHA to partner with employers, workers, professional or trade associations, labor organizations, and/or other interested stakeholders. OSHA Partnerships are formalized through unique agreements designed to encourage, assist, and recognize partner efforts to eliminate serious hazards and achieve model workplace safety and health practices. Through the Alliance Program, OSHA works with groups committed to worker safety and health to prevent workplace fatalities, injuries and illnesses by developing compliance assistance tools and resources to share with workers and employers, and educate workers and employers about their rights and responsibilities.

Voluntary Protection Programs (VPP)

The VPP recognize employers and workers in private industry and federal agencies who have implemented effective safety and health management programs and maintain injury and illness rates below the national average for their respective industries. In VPP, management, labor, and OSHA work cooperatively and proactively to prevent fatalities, injuries, and illnesses through a system focused on: hazard prevention and control, worksite analysis, training, and management commitment and worker involvement.

Occupational Safety and Health Training

The OSHA Training Institute in Arlington Heights, Illinois, provides basic and advanced training and education in safety and health for federal and state compliance officers, state consultants, other federal agency personnel and private sector employers, workers, and their representatives. In addition, 27 OSHA Training Institute Education Centers at 42 locations throughout the United States deliver courses on OSHA standards and occupational safety and health issues to thousands of students a year.

For more information on training, contact the OSHA Directorate of Training and Education, 2020 Arlington Heights Road, Arlington Heights, IL 60005; call 1-847-297-4810; or visit www.osha.gov/otiec.

OSHA Educational Materials

OSHA has many types of educational materials in English, Spanish, Vietnamese and other languages available in print or online. These include:

- Brochures/booklets that cover a wide variety of job hazards and other topics;
- Fact Sheets, which contain basic background information on safety and health hazards;
- Guidance documents that provide detailed examinations of specific safety and health issues;
- Online Safety and Health Topics pages;

- Posters;

- Small, laminated QuickCards™ that provide brief safety and health information; and

- *QuickTakes*, OSHA's free, twice-monthly online newsletter with the latest news about OSHA initiatives and products to assist employers and workers in finding and preventing workplace hazards. To sign up for *QuickTakes* visit www. osha.gov/quicktakes.

To view materials available online or for a listing of free publications, visit www.osha.gov/publications. You can also call 1-800-321-OSHA (6742) to order publications.

OSHA's web site also has a variety of eTools. These include utilities such as expert advisors, electronic compliance assistance, videos and other information for employers and workers. To learn more about OSHA's safety and health tools online, visit www.osha.gov.

NIOSH Health Hazard Evaluation Program

Getting Help with Health Hazards

The National Institute for Occupational Safety and Health (NIOSH) is a federal agency that conducts scientific and medical research on workers' safety and health. At no cost to employers or workers, NIOSH can help identify health hazards and recommend ways to reduce or eliminate those hazards in the workplace through its Health Hazard Evaluation (HHE) Program.

Workers, union representatives and employers can request a NIOSH HHE. An HHE is often requested when there is a higher than expected rate of a disease or injury in a group of workers. These situations may be the result of an unknown cause, a new hazard, or a mixture of sources. To request a NIOSH Health Hazard Evaluation go to www.cdc.gov/niosh/hhe/request.html. To find out more about the Health Hazard Evaluation Program:

- Call (513) 841-4382, or to talk to a staff member in Spanish, call (513) 841-4439; or

- Send an email to HHERequestHelp@cdc.gov.

OSHA Regional Offices

Region I
Boston Regional Office
(CT*, ME, MA, NH, RI, VT*)
JFK Federal Building, Room E340
Boston, MA 02203
(617) 565-9860 (617) 565-9827 Fax

Region II
New York Regional Office
(NJ*, NY*, PR*, VI*)
201 Varick Street, Room 670
New York, NY 10014
(212) 337-2378 (212) 337-2371 Fax

Region III
Philadelphia Regional Office
(DE, DC, MD*, PA, VA*, WV)
The Curtis Center
170 S. Independence Mall West
Suite 740 West
Philadelphia, PA 19106-3309
(215) 861-4900 (215) 861-4904 Fax

Region IV
Atlanta Regional Office
(AL, FL, GA, KY*, MS, NC*, SC*, TN*)
61 Forsyth Street, SW, Room 6T50
Atlanta, GA 30303
(678) 237-0400 (678) 237-0447 Fax

Region V
Chicago Regional Office
(IL*, IN*, MI*, MN*, OH, WI)
230 South Dearborn Street
Room 3244
Chicago, IL 60604
(312) 353-2220 (312) 353-7774 Fax

Region VI
Dallas Regional Office
(AR, LA, NM*, OK, TX)
525 Griffin Street, Room 602
Dallas, TX 75202
(972) 850-4145 (972) 850-4149 Fax
(972) 850-4150 FSO Fax

Region VII
Kansas City Regional Office
(IA*, KS, MO, NE)
Two Pershing Square Building
2300 Main Street, Suite 1010
Kansas City, MO 64108-2416
(816) 283-8745 (816) 283-0547 Fax

Region VIII
Denver Regional Office
(CO, MT, ND, SD, UT*, WY*)
Cesar Chavez Memorial Building
1244 Speer Boulevard, Suite 551
Denver, CO 80204
(720) 264-6550 (720) 264-6585 Fax

Region IX
San Francisco Regional Office
(AZ*, CA*, HI*, NV*, and American Samoa,
Guam and the Northern Mariana Islands)
90 7th Street, Suite 18100
San Francisco, CA 94103
(415) 625-2547 (415) 625-2534 Fax
Region X
Seattle Regional Office
(AK*, ID, OR*, WA*)
300 Fifth Avenue, Suite 1280
Seattle, WA 98104
(206) 757-6700 (206) 757-6705 Fax

* These states and territories operate their own OSHA-approved job safety and health plans and cover state and local government employees as well as private sector employees. The Connecticut, Illinois, New Jersey, New York and Virgin Islands programs cover public employees only. (Private sector workers in these states are covered by Federal OSHA). States with approved programs must have standards that are identical to, or at least as effective as, the Federal OSHA standards.

Note: To get contact information for OSHA area offices, OSHA-approved state plans and OSHA consultation projects, please visit us online at www.osha.gov or call us at 1-800-321-OSHA (6742).

How to Contact OSHA

For questions or to get information or advice, to report an emergency, report a fatality or catastrophe, order publications, sign up for OSHA's e-newsletter *QuickTakes*, or to file a confidential complaint, contact your nearest OSHA office, visit www.osha.gov or call OSHA at 1-800-321-OSHA (6742), TTY 1-877-889-5627.

**For assistance, contact us.
We are OSHA. We can help.**